To Lea

with all a

Best wishes

[handwritten signature]

1

Discovering the Gifts Within

Christine Pham French

With Samantha Glauser

3

Cover: lotus flower

The lotus (*Hoa Sen* in Vietnamese) is the national flower of Vietnam. It symbolizes beauty, majesty, grace, fertility, wealth, richness, knowledge, and serenity, representing the human spirit.

The magnificent lotus flowers emerge from the dirty and murky bottom of a pond, and yet remain untouched by all the dirt and mud of the environment, in which it grows.

The flower also contains many gifts within. Every part of the lotus can be used to make food or medicine. Lotus seeds are used to make candy, *mứt hạt sen*; tea, *chè hat sen*; and so on. Lotus leaves are used to wrap food. Lotus roots are used to make medicine and various kinds of food.

6

Table of Contents

Acknowledgments

First and foremost, thank you to my Father for giving me everything I need and teaching me everything I know.

Grateful thanks

- To my parents, who gave me life and taught me the unending wisdom of our Asian culture.

- To my husband Phil, for opening the door to my career path, where I learned the ever-changing business practices. I am grateful for your love and support through many activities with the family. You are my best "life gift" and I love you.

- To my daughters Claire and Paula, who enriched my life with their brilliant minds, generous hearts, and enough mischief to keep me grounded.

- To my grandsons Alexandre, Christian, Noah, and Ethan, who taught me to live one day at a time and enjoy the presents they are to me and the family.

- To my colleagues and all the people who work hard to make the world a better place for providing opportunities for me to blend the wisdom of the Eastern and Western cultures as we identified and applied solutions to achieve their business goals in this turbulent time.

- To my editors, Paige Lehnert and Angie Kiesling for making sure this book is "fit to print."

Preface

"I have a book in me. Will you write it?"

It started out simply enough. I knew Christine through a friend and had met her on several occasions. A wonderful and beautiful person, she was very easy to talk with. She had an innate curiosity about people and a desire to get to know you and to understand you along with the ability to draw you out. She had a warm and positive energy packed into a five-foot-tall body.

While I knew a little bit about her from our mutual friend, I admit I was curious. "A book? About what?" I asked.

My question led to an adventure in which I learned so much about this amazing woman and her passion for diversity through her wonderful stories. I thought I understood diversity and recognized it as the differences between people: age, gender, color, race, and religion, among others. However, through our discussions I learned that diversity is so much more: diversity is not only how people are different, but also how we are the same. It's about respect, learning and opening minds. It's about life itself and how we live it, as Christine says. Our success depends on how we manage our lives with all of the positive things that happen, as well as how we manage the challenges.

Working on this book has also caused me to look at success a little differently, too. It has opened my eyes to recognizing the differences and similarities in all people, regardless of what they look like on the outside. I better appreciate who I am and who the people are who surround me. I now define success more in terms of personal fulfillment and the enrichment that comes with the process of seeking it, as opposed to the more traditional definitions.

Although Christine grew up across the world from me in Vietnam, in talking with her I gained some of the most powerful learning, knowledge, and insights I have ever known. I am proud to now call Christine a friend.

—Samantha Glauser

Introduction

What is diversity? According to Merriam-Webster, *diversity* is defined as "the condition of being diverse: the inclusion of diverse people (as people of different races or cultures) in a group or organization." Wikipedia defines *diversity* as "the business tactic that encourages diversity to better serve a heterogeneous customer base." Dictionary.com defines *diversity* similarly, as "1. The state or fact of being diverse; difference; unlikeness. 2. Variety, multiformity. 3. A point of difference."

In traditional definitions around the world, people think about race, religion, and gender, typically in a professional context. Diversity is so much more than that: it is how each of us is different and how we are the same. It is how we connect, appreciate, and respect each other, and most importantly, how we think, act, and behave when things are not what we expect, are not familiar, or when we don't agree with them. People are all unique individuals and cannot be categorized based on simple attributes. Diversity is about all of us; it's the expression of life.

Diversity is life itself. It is the way we express ourselves and all that we are. We're all uniquely different from each other, and it's important to understand those differences in order to be successful both in business and in life. I have twins in my family, and though they were born at the same time and of the same parents, they are incredibly different people. They share a very similar face, but the individuals beneath that exterior share little in terms of personality.

In a work setting, when we hire people, for example, we often hire those we feel a connection with or who we think agree with us, see our viewpoints, and share our principles. Or maybe they went to the same school as we did, so we feel a connection. However, these similarities don't really provide any frame of reference for how someone will perform. These commonalities don't mean we have the same intelligence, the same experience level, and the same abilities. By looking for the common links, we are making sweeping assumptions about a person and we are overlooking a lot.

If you are the head of an IT team, for example, you will evaluate a candidate's technical competency to determine if they are a good fit for your team and for your position. What about people who are different from you? Will you be able to judge their technical competency when what you are looking at is so different from you and what you are familiar with? You may be expecting a young white male or perhaps a young Indian male. What if a 50-year-old woman walked in? Would you be able to evaluate her abilities and see beyond her appearance? What if the woman was very young and looked like she might not be old enough to have graduated college? Or what if an older man arrived in a wheelchair? It's so important to recognize the role our expectations play in decision-making, to ensure we are not overlooking quality candidates who are a good fit just because the package doesn't appear as we expect it to.

An understanding of the importance of diversity is not only important with hiring decisions but also with retention, employee satisfaction, and productivity. When I worked for a Fortune 100 company and traveled the world educating people about the value of diversity and inclusion, I was told, "We don't have that problem here. That's the American problem." Their understanding was that in America, where there was a women's movement and where slavery was depicted in the colors of black and white, diversity was an American issue and not a global one.

When people come to me with issues, I take a different approach and focus on the person instead. "The purpose of our conversation is to talk about you. What are your strengths, challenges, and aspirations, and what is keeping you from achieving your life's goal?" During the discussion, we often find out that which is keeping them from achieving their goal is the "system." They often say, "We don't do *this* in..." or "It's always done this way..." or "that's not the way we do it here..." This is essentially calling out the organization's culture as a factor, and we need to pay attention to that. Who are "we" and who put a stop to us pursuing our dreams? People forget to take ownership of their own life and allow others to define who they are instead of defining who they are and what they wish to be themselves.

I'm often asked how I got into diversity and inclusion work, and when I answer, I think back to the day of my birth. It was March 13, 1944, and a day marked by steady bombing. Japan was bombing Hanoi, and my family lived in the outskirts of Hanoi. My parents, along with hundreds of other people, ran to seek the protection of the Redemptorist Church in Nam Dong, which was run by Canadian priests. They were all hiding in the basement of the church where I was born a short time later.

I was born dead: I was blue and not breathing at all. My father ran to find a doctor and was unable to find anyone except for a retired French doctor, who was very old and almost blind. The doctor grabbed me by a leg and literally beat the life into me. Finally, I let out a yell, the first sign that I might make it. My father said he was unsure whether to hug him or slug him since my little body was covered with welts. The doctor couldn't see me, so he just kept hitting me until I cried!

My dad named me Christine after Saint Christine, a young Italian girl who was martyred when she was only thirteen years old. I was born on the thirteenth. My parents never spoke to me about the day of my birth, though I did learn the story of the experience. As I grew up, my parents never said anything to me about why I was saved when I was born.

Why *was* I saved that day? I still remember when people would ask, "How's the family?" my parents would say, "Thank you. Our family is well. Except for our older daughter. Would you please pray for her?" I wondered why I was so bad that they would make that request, and it haunted me for years.

The year I turned fifty, I had a revelation. My youngest daughter had just turned twenty-five, and we were talking about her life, and specifically, her calling. She was questioning what she was meant to do with her life. Then and there, the realization came to me. The reason my parents asked people to pray for me was not because I was bad or sick; it was because so many people died that day and I was spared. There had to be a reason for my living, but they didn't know what it was, so they asked people to pray for me with the hope that I would find my life purpose someday.

Then I understood there was a reason I had been spared. I had a life mission to fulfill and I needed to find what it was. I may have known deep down and I had some ideas, however, I only vaguely knew and I couldn't articulate it at the time. If people asked me what I liked to do, I always said I liked to encourage people and to help them believe in themselves. It was not until a few years later, as I went deeper into my diversity work, that I realized my full mission: to validate people and to educate them in order to motivate them.

So many people believe that others know what they are called to do in life. Many of these people have a vague idea, however, it takes work to be able to delve deeper in order to articulate it. I truly believe each one of us is called to do something significant. I was plucked from a third world country and "dropped" in a small town in the Unites States to be loved and nurtured before I was sent out in the world to share all I'd learned from my experiences.

I was called to validate people because we often forget how powerful we are. Each of us is called to do something different, and we learn what our calling is when we are fortunate enough to have time to do the personal work required. My diversity work has been a gift, and I reap the satisfaction of knowing I am helping people.

You may or may not agree with me as to how I define the word *diversity*, however, I encourage you to keep your mind open. Continue reading to discover the richness and strength of this often misunderstood word and how taking a wider view of the definition can add to your life. At the end of this book, I hope you come up with your own personal definition, which will be the most important of all. When you discover all of this, you will appreciate all that you are so much more.

This book is dedicated to the thousands of people devoted to the work of diversity and inclusion and to ensure that everyone is equally respected, empowered, and appreciated.

—Christine Pham French

Chapter 1

Unexpected Gifts

I was twenty-three when I moved to the United States from Vietnam. During my first year in the country, I visited my fiancée's town of Reinbeck, Iowa. Reinbeck consisted of just over a thousand people, mostly farmers of Germanic and of European descent. The family that welcomed me was tall, dark-haired, and fair-skinned—a stark contrast to me.

The entire family greeted me at the door, eager to meet the woman who was soon to be the newest member of their family. I was overwhelmed by their warm welcome, as I had been so afraid they would not accept me since I wasn't from there. I asked everyone to please sit down. "After all," I said, "I don't want to talk to your belt buckles!" My acknowledgment of our obvious differences helped to break the ice.

They asked me about my parents, my family, and where I was from. They also wanted to know how old I was because I looked so young and they found it hard to believe I was old enough to be marrying.

My husband's grandfather was a doctor. He looked at me, watching from the back of the crowd, saying little at first. It was as if he just didn't know what to make of me. Then he made a statement that I will remember forever: "She has nice teeth, so she must be okay." Then the rest of the family joined in. "She's so cute!" they said. Relieved to find out that my future in-laws did not hate me, though curious about their reaction to me, I found myself feeling right at home due to some of the similarities between the small town of Reinbeck and where I was from. After all, Vietnam was an agricultural country, so I was familiar with farming. In Vietnam, when a young man reached the age for marriage, his parents would select a healthy young woman for him who could help with the farm work. A weak, sickly girl would not do.

My in-laws' comments made me think about the similarities and connections, even across the world. I realized we weren't so different after all, and my recognition of our similarities made me feel comfortable. At the same time, the "rebellious child" in me started to whisper in my ear. Did they think he brought home a pet? I was being inspected as an animal would be in Vietnam: when you bought a pet, you looked at its teeth to determine health. This told you if it had been well cared for and if it came from good stock. At the same time, I didn't feel that they meant offense, as I could feel the warmth emanating from them. Finding the similarities helped to ease my loneliness and missing my family.

My mother-in-law was a wonderful person, and I know it was important to her that I felt welcomed and accepted by her community. I later learned that prior to meeting me, she had asked everyone she knew to offer hospitality to make me feel welcome. My in-laws were very well connected in the community, as my father-in-law was the town's funeral director. She asked all of her friends, her bridge and sewing clubs, and the church to show me the hospitality that the town had to offer because I was here alone and had no family.

But I was not truly alone; I had my whole world with me. Though my family wasn't with me, their teachings and guidance, my culture, and my way of life always remained with me. All of my actions were as if they were right there with me, guiding my way. It was mostly self-preservation; when you don't know anyone on whom you can depend, you maintain a strong connection to those you care about for your peace of mind and security. When I didn't know how to respond to certain things, I would imagine my mom standing right in front of me, and with her guidance, I'd find my response.

Most people really made an effort to ensure that we felt welcomed. Initially, I felt they did it more out of curiosity than genuine caring, and I felt almost like a monkey in a zoo. I added quite a bit of color to the town, in more ways than one! There were no people of color in the town, so my arrival caught people off-guard. Many people told me that when they heard I was marrying into the family, they were surprised, as they expected a "light beauty" and not a "dark beauty."

I was in the midst of a culture shock, and everything was so new. I was meeting many new people whose names I struggled to pronounce, and I was trying to understand everything that was going on around me. Slowly things changed as people became accustomed to me and I to them.

My in-laws did a wonderful job ensuring I was welcomed; however, I didn't go unchallenged. While it was never outwardly stated, I learned that any time a country is at war the "war brides" are not appreciated or valued by some. This includes a relationship with a person from the country that the United States is at war with, and not just those brought back during the war from that country. Given my father-in-law's status in the community, most people wouldn't overtly disrespect me, but I felt it on occasion.

My husband and I were invited to people's homes, and we continued to be invited with every return visit. For those who accepted me with open arms, I returned the warmth. I tried to show that their acceptance meant so much to me in my own way. One of those ways was through eye contact. Americans value eye contact and it signifies different things: respect, caring, attention.

However, in Vietnam, eye contact had a completely different meaning: it was reserved for people with a relationship. If you wish to demonstrate respect in Vietnam, you lower your head. If you raise your head and make eye contact, particularly with a person of the opposite gender, it carried the meaning of flirtation or a sexual connotation. It also could signify a challenge or confrontation. While I found it difficult to make eye contact, I understood how important it was and the meaning that it conveyed in this country, so I made the effort to do so. I enthusiastically used both hands to shake their hand while maintaining eye contact.

The Vietnam War ended for the United States in 1975 when troops withdrew from Vietnam. I feared for my family, which remained in Vietnam. One morning a couple of weeks after the end of United States involvement, my father-in-law approached me holding an envelope. "Chrisso," as he called me, "I've got something for you." I opened the envelope to find a check for $30,000. I looked up at him, not understanding. "Buy the airline tickets and bring your family here," he declared. Without my knowledge, he had taken out a bank loan using his funeral home business as collateral.

"Don't worry about paying it back," he said. I was speechless. My eyes filled with tears and I had a lump in my throat. This was not about obligation, but love: it was because of me and our relationship that he took out a significant loan against the family business to save my family. I was no longer this "cute little thing" from Vietnam, but their daughter-in-law, and someone they loved and wanted to protect.

My family arrived the first week of May.

Chapter 2

Different Worlds

People generally follow the cultures and tradition of their families and those around them in the community. Though diversity is usually considered in a work context, it impacts the personal aspects of our daily life as well. Recognizing differences is a personal experience, and an understanding or an awareness of the differences that we have from those around us can greatly benefit us.

Life in Vietnam was different than life in the United States in so many ways. In Vietnam, I wouldn't want my mother to go into the kitchen and I would do everything needed so I could take care of her. I did all the cooking and the cleaning as a way to honor my mother and to show her the respect that, as my mother and my elder, she deserved. This was expected in Vietnam.

My mother began teaching me at a young age what was expected of a girl in that society. I was taught to take care of my family and to serve them. At the age of five, I was sent to school to learn to sew while my brother went outside to play. One day I put on his shirt and said I was a boy so I wouldn't have to go to school.

By the time I was nine years old, I was sent to the market every day to get vegetables, groceries, and other items. I attended school every morning and then in the afternoon I went to the market to get food for the evening meal. When I arrived home, my mother would teach me to cook. There were no cookbooks and I learned by doing it and by tasting what I made. I knew my place in my family and in my society.

There is a saying in Vietnam: "If I have to tell you I love you, I have failed." Actions always were believed to speak louder than words. My mother never expressed her feelings but showed me in her own way. I had one set of clothes as a child that I washed and ironed every morning before I went out. My mother would keep an eye on the dress to determine when it was time to buy me a new one. Buying a dress in Vietnam was a big deal then because clothes were custom tailored. My mother had to buy material, take my measurements, and go to a tailor to have the dress made. So my mother showed her love by taking care of me and ensuring I never needed anything. Of course, I didn't always see it at the time, as sometimes our subtle actions are lost.

My mother died in 1973 while I was living in Michigan. When I knew she was going to have surgery, I applied for a visa to go home to visit. Unfortunately, I didn't make it in time, and she died the day before my visa was approved.

Following tradition, they put her in the freezer to wait until all the immediate family came home. As soon as I arrived, I went directly to the morgue, where we had a ceremony of preparation. They did not, and still do not, have funeral homes in Vietnam, so the immediate family was responsible for all preparations. We washed her, clothed her in the dress she asked to be buried in, and then we wrapped her in brand new cotton cloth. After we wrapped my mom tightly in layers of cloth, we laid her in a metal box packed with dried tea leaves and then welded the box shut so it was airtight. We then laid her in an unadorned coffin with no satin, filling, pillows, or any other decoration. It was just a simple wooden box, nicely carved on the outside. The coffin was again packed with dried tea leaves and then nailed shut.

The immediate family dressed in white loose cotton and gauze mourning clothes. Headpieces defined the relationship with the deceased. As the daughter, I wore a long white gauze hood that covered my face in the front and trailed down to my legs in the back. I wore sandals made of straw. My brothers wore a white band made of gauze around their heads with a tail down to the middle of their backs. Cousins, brothers, and sisters of the deceased didn't wear the white garment but did wear a white headpiece either of the male or female version. Only immediate children had headpieces of gauze, and the rest of the family wore headpieces of cotton.

We brought my mother home for three days so our family and friends could pay their last respects. Mostly people wore black, except for the immediate family members who wore white. No bright colors were worn. When visitors came, they expected to be fed by the family. A sit-down meal was prepared and cooked. The belief was that since the visitors came to pay their respects to your family member, you needed to show appreciation and respect by taking care of them.

After three days, we took her to the church for the last service and then we took her to the cemetery. We rented taxis and cars for the guests, and the immediate children all walked. I was ten weeks pregnant and my sister was seven months pregnant. No accommodations were made for us because hospitality was more important than anything else.

After my mother was placed in the ground and covered with dirt and flowers, many people returned to the family's house for a meal. I was feeling rebellious, so instead of going home, I took my family to the beach for a week before coming home. There were a lot of people we never saw when my mother was alive, so when she died and there were gatherings, they all arrived. I decided it was more important for us to go away somewhere instead of taking care of everyone else.

My relationship with my mother-in-law was so different, as was her funeral. My mother-in-law often told me she loved me and appreciated me. I remember many times over my first year of marriage that my mother-in-law not only did special things for me, but she would also hold my hands and tell me how happy she was to have me in her life.

The first summer after I was married, I moved to New Jersey. My in-laws came for a visit and stayed for a couple of weeks. I went to work and when I arrived back home, my mother-in-law had cleaned my apartment from top to bottom. She had even taken the entire stove apart to clean it, as I didn't know how! The entire apartment was spotless!

I was quite embarrassed, however, she explained that she did it to do something nice for me and not because she felt she needed to. She then taught me how to clean the stove so I could do it myself. In Vietnam, the kitchen was outside and we didn't have appliances like we did in the United States. Instead of criticizing me and making me feel bad, my mother-in-law taught me by example and trained me how to do things. Since she had no daughters, I was treated like her daughter and my relationship with her was special.

After she left my house, she went into the hospital for one hundred days. My husband and I went back to Iowa to interview for jobs in order to move there. We went to visit her in the hospital, and one time I went alone. She asked me to come closer and held my head to her chest, telling me how happy she was that I was her daughter-in-law. She had made me so happy and made me feel so loved, and I thanked her for welcoming me into her family so warmly. It was the most wonderful thing I'd ever experienced: to be told I was loved, and to be able to fully reciprocate that love. I cried from the depth of my being, as I knew these would be her last words to me. She died shortly after my visit.

Everything was done so differently than it was in Vietnam. None of us dressed her, as that was the embalmer's job. We did select her clothes, though someone else tended to her. The casket was open and had white satin pillows and padding with beautiful embroidery. "Oh, she's so beautiful," people said, and, "She looks like she's asleep." It was all very elaborate, and it felt as if we were in denial. We had a wake and then the funeral three days later. The entire town arrived with food, which I thought was such a wonderful custom because it gave people the opportunity to show us how much they cared about my mother-in-law by taking care of her family.

I was overcome by grief at the thought of never seeing her again on the drive to the cemetery. When I cried out in anguish, I was shushed. I never felt as out-of-place in the United States as I did that day. I felt as if my grief was being denied. At the funeral, everyone was in perfect control. Whenever I cried, I was shushed. I was really upset by her loss and because culturally things were so different and I was unable to express those emotions.

In Vietnam, emotion is not expressed as freely as it is in the United States, however, it's accepted to wail and cry when someone you care about dies. My mother-in-law died on October 30, and the ground was frozen for the burial. The grave was dug and beams were laid across the grave so the casket could rest on it. After the church service, the casket was brought out, a few words were said, and people left. I was absolutely horrified to just leave her there alone. In Vietnam, it's the children's task to see to it that a loved one is fully taken care of before they leave. I thought, 'Wait! We can't leave her there!' however, everyone left and I had no choice. She was lowered without anyone in her family in attendance.

I felt like we were all in denial. People talked of her "passing away" instead of "dying" as if they were denying what happened. The phrases people used were so confusing. Americans are a culture of immediacy and the living, of here and now. However, interestingly, people in Vietnam don't deal with death until the time comes like they do in America. In America, people buy insurance and prepare for their death, whereas in Vietnam, it's simply understood that the family will take care of it when the time comes. This was such a clash with my culture that I had a really hard time with it.

The funerals for both my mother and my mother-in-law were so different. Each followed the respect and tradition of the culture in which they lived. Understanding the differences is a personal experience. I had no teacher and had to learn as I went through experience. We often think of diversity in a work context, though it impacts our everyday life as well. Not understanding this or not recognizing it can bring pain.

Chapter 3

Understanding
Authority and Culture

As we grow up, we learn about different situations where we strive to understand influence and power. An understanding of cultural differences and influences can have a significant impact on what we learn and how effective that learning is in driving our successful behavior dealing with different people.

When I was six years old, I attended my first day of school. Vietnam was a French colony at the time, and given my parent's social standing in the community, I was able to attend a French school.

I remember sitting in a class at the front of the room listening to the teacher, like all of the other students. The teacher said to repeat after him, "My country is France, and my hero is Charlemagne." But how could that be? We were in Vietnam, not France, and Charlemagne was of no importance here.

As only a six-year-old—like I was at the time—would do, I shouted out my disagreement. "No we're not!" I cried. "This is Vietnam." I was sitting in the front row right on the aisle, so the teacher made it to my desk in a few steps. Shocked by my outburst and without saying a word, he raised his hand and brought it hard against my face, back-handing me. I had spoken out of turn, disagreeing with him, and it was not to be tolerated. Children simply did not question an adult.

As I grew up I learned that the teachers, as with all other people in a position of power, were inherently right. As a child, I was not allowed to disagree with a statement made by a teacher. We were taught $2+2=4$. Anything else was incorrect.

I learned on that day what it was to "lose face." When my teacher's hand met my face, my world went dark. I could not see anything and my face felt hot and swollen. I couldn't breathe, and I ceased to exist. It was a frightening experience and very unpleasant. I was no longer there in that room, and I felt like I no longer existed.

People talk about not wanting to lose face or not wanting to make other people feel that way, but so few people truly understand. At the young age of six, I did. I learned that painful lesson of what it means to lose face and how it feels when it happens. It was frightening, it was painful, and it was awful. Even today I go out of my way to ensure other people don't lose face. I try to rescue people so they do not feel like that six-year-old child once did.

My mother picked me up at school. Of course, I could not tell her what happened because then I would be in bigger trouble. The teacher was the supreme power in school, so if the teacher said I was wrong, then I was. My culture, and many Asian cultures at that time, believed people should not get out of line. There were certain social norms such that you must adhere to. There was an expectation of "law and order," where everything fits and has its perfect place. People in a position of power, like a teacher, are always right. I would have been punished if I told my mother what happened. So instead I carried the shame of what I had done with me, and it's a lesson I have never lost.

If we take this logic to the workplace, when you manage people and a team member disagrees, naturally they are wrong. As the leader, you know better. You've been there longer, you've been more successful, and you're in power, so you are right as the leader. Do we miss out on opportunities to hear other perspectives with this logic? Do we cheat ourselves of being exposed to other thoughts and ideas that we had not thought of or had not experienced because they are not in line with what we believe to be right?

If anything out of the norm is wrong, then don't we miss out on new ideas with this belief system? This happens all the time.

The challenge of diversity, along with the beauty and strength of it, is the enrichment that we get: when we are open to it, we see many different perspectives and ways to enjoy each other and life. Differences enrich us with varied perspectives and many ways to view situations or to solve problems. There are so many ways of doing most anything, but we have a tendency to look at new or different things negatively. If we haven't heard of it, then it must be wrong or it must not be. People who disagree with us, well, they must be wrong. If we have not experienced it, then it's strange or weird. But when we take a step back and open our minds to different thoughts and perspectives, it opens a door to a whole new way of looking at things and increases our opportunities for success.

I traveled to Japan with the general manager of my business to meet with a potential customer. The leader, whom we traveled to meet, saw me and rushed over to greet me. He had met me before and warmly welcomed me back to Japan. He did not look at or acknowledge in any way my boss, the general manager, who stood at my side.

Once he left, my boss expressed his anger and frustration. "What was that about? Why didn't you introduce us?" I explained to him that the reason he was not acknowledged was because he had not yet been introduced. In the local culture, a person must be formally introduced to someone in order to be acknowledged. Further, he must be formally introduced to exist, and we had not done that and had not established his role. My boss did not appreciate this at all and told me "that's a stupid custom!" I am not sure if anybody heard it, but we did lose the contract.

When we deal with high context cultures, where fewer words are spoken but a high meaning is attributed to what is said, people learn to listen to both the spoken word and also to what is not spoken. Body language is very important. The English language is considered "low context," so the ways of business are very different from how business is done in other parts of the world. For example, Americans use more words in their communications than their global counterparts. The roles people play are also very different in meetings.

A typical business meeting in America may have a few minutes of "small talk" and then they "get down to business." So in the case of contract negotiations, an American will often bring up the contract pretty quickly in the meeting to establish its importance and to move things forward.

In other parts of the world, business is conducted a little differently. The leader never talks about money; that's the task for the lower ranks to discuss. In negotiation, the leader talks about the vision and the junior people discuss the details of the contract. As a guest, you should never bring up the contract but let the host do so. Sometimes this could take several days. While Americans view time as money and want to get down to business, other cultures perceive this impatience as disrespect.

Another example can be seen while dining. In Asia, you don't say to a waiter, "I need more tea." Instead, it's much more subtle to remove the lid on the teapot to let the waiter know you would like your tea to be filled. To thank the waiter, you don't take attention away from your guest. Instead, you tap two fingers on the table. Taking time away from your guest to interact with a waiter is perceived as disrespect, while an American might view this exchange as being discourteous to the waiter.

In the American culture, some of us may take potential employees to play golf so we can observe their actions to evaluate if they would fit on our team. We may also do this when evaluating someone for a promotion or in evaluating a business deal. It's a form of testing. Americans are not the only culture to test others. Other countries and other cultures do it all the time, and sometimes we miss it. It's important to understand this and the tests of other countries to be able to succeed. Other cultures know Americans are impatient, so they purposely test us by seeing how we control our emotions and how we act and react. Understanding this puts us in a place of strength so we can be successful.

Chapter 4

Gaps in Understanding

We interpret the new things that happen in our world based on our past experiences. This is further influenced by our cultural interpretations. Though this initial interpretation may be useful, it can lead us to the wrong conclusions. Reaching out to understand people and to determine the meaning behind their actions can help us to bridge the gap between cultures.

After a couple of weeks in Reinbeck, Iowa, with my fiancée's family, I felt that most people there genuinely loved and accepted me for who I was, including my new family. I do believe that any feelings of insecurity were my own due to my lack of understanding American culture. However, it was apparent that the difference in cultures, and more specifically my lack of understanding of American culture, would provide some challenges and misunderstandings in my new life.

My in-laws were wonderful and offered to provide me with a full traditional wedding, which was truly a wonderful gift. Some close family friends offered to throw me a bridal shower. This was quite a culture shock, as it was not a custom done in Vietnam. It was important for me to be accepted into my new family, and I was so appreciative of all that they did to accept me, that I went along with it.

However, I was anxious because I was not sure what a bridal shower was. I thought perhaps it was what was done in some Buddhist cultures, where it was a purification ceremony and maybe a bath. This is customary in many Asian cultures as well where, before any major life event, there is a spiritual and physical purification. The bride and groom go to different places in a temple for anywhere from three days to a week to have the purification of mind, body, and spirit. There is meditation and water cleansing where your family splashes you with water. In some places deep in the jungle, an elephant might even spray you with water.

In Asian cultures, there is a belief that no woman can ever be good enough for your son. In some cultures upon marriage, the groom's family would give the bride a whipping to ensure her obedience and to teach her who is in charge through fear. While I didn't know anyone who'd had it done to them, it was part of the Asian culture and what's talked about.

I was familiar with the Disney movies, like *Cinderella*, which showcased the wicked stepmother, and it all became intertwined in my head. I had no idea what to expect of the bridal shower, and my lack of familiarity with American customs as well as some of the rumored traditions in some Asian cultures had me confused and concerned.

I arrived to see a beautiful spread of food and a large table covered with presents. As I scanned the table, I saw a rod for a shower curtain. It was a long wooden rod, and it became the symbol of all of my wildest fears. I was sure I was going to be beaten with this wooden rod.

I was asked to sit and open my presents. My fiancé was not there, as no men were invited to the shower, so I couldn't ask him what to expect. My anxiety level grew as I opened the gifts of linens, towels, and everything I could want for my new house. All I could think was, "When are they going to do it? Will they beat me here or will they take me outside? Why are they torturing me with waiting? The rugs are so thick; it must be to muffle my cries." It was all I could do to get through the event without running out because where would I run? Where could I go when there were so many people at the shower, all smiling and laughing and looking so happy? I could not understand why they all seemed so happy when I was about to be beaten.

I don't know how I made it through the shower, but I did. The last gift was the shower rod. It was handed over to me and I thought "OK. This is it, now." I had resigned myself to my fate and wanted to get it over with. The place the shower was held at was a farm five miles from the next house. I couldn't run and I had nowhere to go, so I prepared myself for what was to come.

My husband's grandmother came over to me and said, "Let's go home!" to which I replied with tears in my eyes, "Home? Is that it?" She looked very surprised. "Wasn't that enough? Did you expect more?" My mother-in-law laughed at first and said, "Yes, isn't this enough? We won't fit any more in our car!" Then she saw the look on my face and realized what had been going through my mind during the entire shower.

She had worked so hard to welcome me, and she had read extensively about Vietnam to try to understand me. However, all of her efforts did not in any way prepare her for my interpretation of the shower, and she did not understand what I feared through the entire day. When she looked at me and saw the raw fear on my face, her eyes filled with tears and she hugged me. She had no idea that for the last few hours, I was stiff with fear of being beaten with the shower rod.

Cultural differences can bring a lot of pain when you don't understand them.

During my first trip to India for a corporate business trip, we stayed at a Hilton, a very rich and beautiful hotel overlooking the water. It was really amazing. I looked out of the windows of my room and felt like I was floating on the water. There were huge pillars in the courtyard with fire at night and a huge pool of water at the entrance with four pillars of fire around it and one in the center in the middle of a pool of water. At night it was a most magnificent picture.

The hotel grounds were gated, and just outside the gate lived the poorest of the poor people. There were families living on top of a garbage heap as large as several buildings and as tall as a ten- to fifteen-story building. You could see the tents on top of the heap of garbage where the people lived.

The women of India were dressed in beautiful saris. Even those living on top of the garbage heap wore gorgeous in their flowing and colorful saris. They did not wear shoes if they could not afford them, and many went barefoot. The flash of color and beauty was such a stark contrast to their living conditions. It was also a further contrast to the opulent hotel I was staying in which, though right next door, felt like it was worlds away.

India had been a colony of Great Britain. The British built bridges and schools when they were there, as well as infrastructure in the country. These structures became targets for resistance, and people would destroy these British contributions to the country in a sign of defiance. "This is not ours, so we don't want it" was the belief of the resistance.

There were many huge companies developing giant buildings all over due to the economic growth in the country. Many of these buildings were more than twenty or thirty stories, and they had to excavate the ground below for adequate support. However, there was nowhere to place the dirt, so they often moved it nearby in large piles. When the rains came, the dirt turned to mud and slid down the hills, becoming hazardous to the inhabitants of the area.

One day I left my corporate office at 5:30 and took a taxi to my hotel. It rained that day, and it was like a downpour, a really hard shower. A river of mud ran down the roads, and the usual fifteen-minute ride to the hotel took more than three-and-a-half hours because we were unable to move. There were cars, bikes, trucks, and mopeds strewn all over the road. While we had some safety inside the car, it was a truly frightening experience. We wanted to get out of the car to walk, but we didn't dare. We were so afraid that the rush of water and mud would come and sweep us away.

My travel companion, Lisa, was a blonde American woman, and the locals were very intrigued by her blonde hair. They would knock on the taxi doors and windows to take a good look at her. Sometimes when we had no place to go, they would surround and literally shake the car. We were often afraid we would get turned over by the mobs of people that gathered around the car. We didn't understand what the people were actually saying by their actions. They were curious and appreciative of our differences, and they just wanted to be near us. But since we didn't understand, it was scary.

It happened on the day of the rain as well. All of these faces were pressed against our windows, shaking the car to get her to look at them. It was truly frightening. We often fear the unknown and view it negatively. We didn't understand the culture and were scared of what was going on.

The car was surrounded by a sea of dark faces. It was then that I had a realization. As we were sitting in the back of the cab in fear that we might get swept away by the rushing waters, I said to my colleague, "No. I did not come to India to die needlessly. I have a mission to do in life and my mission is not finished. So I *will* get back to that hotel and nothing bad will happen to us today."

Then I thought back to my bridal shower, where I was fearful because I didn't understand what was going on around me. "Aha," I said. "This is another situation where understanding the culture and the meaning of actions will help me to not be scared." Reaching out, even figuratively, to understand other people and the intent behind their actions can help us to bridge the gap between cultures and to interpret things in a more positive way.

Chapter 5

Education About
Differences

Humility and respect go a long way in building new relationships and in understanding different people. Recognition, validation, education, and communication are key to ensuring that you listen with an open ear, an open mind, and an open heart.

When I was eight, we learned about social studies in school. We talked about ambassadors and their role as diplomats between countries. I raised my hand, stood up, and told the teacher I was going to be an ambassador someday. Everyone laughed. As a little girl in Vietnam at the time, it was as remote and unlikely as someone in America saying they were going to be queen.

The image has followed me wherever I go. In any situation, I'd think, "What would an ambassador do? How would they respond?" To this day, I feel I truly *am* an ambassador. The role of an ambassador is to spread understanding between countries. When they do their job well, they can prevent war. And for someone born in the midst of war, this was very important to me.

A lot of times in conflict situations, even now in my mind, I still hear the question, "What would an ambassador do?" Most of the time I don't react to it, but I will stop to think and will respond accordingly to the situation.

As a child, I realized how important it was to ask questions, and to ask those questions well before making recommendations for improvement. I wasn't ever taught this, but it was always there. It was given to me. Once I accepted my role as an ambassador, I was able to realize the gifts that came with effectively playing out the role. In part, I gained the wording and mannerisms to help prevent some pain resulting from misunderstanding.

One instance, I had a chance to assume the role of ambassador when I lived in Peoria, Illinois, in 1968, during the Tet

Offensive in the Vietnam War. Many Americans were injured or killed, and hostility in this country built to the point where it was palpable. Having come from Vietnam, I was invited to many churches and schools to talk with people about Vietnam.

On one particular day, I was asked to talk to a women's group because their fathers, brothers, and sons were in Vietnam fighting in the war. Some of the crowd was openly hostile, and several people angrily pointed their fingers at me, saying, "My son is in Vietnam. Why are you here?" They had a hard time understanding why their loved ones were across the world in the country of my birth fighting for my people's freedom while I was living in the United States. Their thinking was that I should be at home in Vietnam fighting my own country's war.

Their anger really hit me hard. For a few seconds, my world went dark, just as it did when I was six years old and had "lost face" in the classroom. I felt shame. While I understood their anger and pain, I knew I had an important task to do: I was to be the ambassador that I connected with at age eight. For reasons I cannot explain, I connected with the ambassador of my childhood and then considered what one would do in this situation. While the crowd's anger was clearly directed at me, it was based on emotions of fear and confusion. So could I help to make their loved ones' experiences more real by connecting them?

I opened my eyes and looked at the crowd. I could hear the words I said next, but I didn't feel as if they came from me. I was twenty-four at the time and didn't have a lot of life experience to draw from. But my "inner ambassador" took over and showed me the way.

I said, "Thank you for asking that question and for giving me the opportunity to share with you and to respond. I can imagine how much you have missed your loved ones in Vietnam. I know because I'm here and my family is back home in Vietnam. There are days I miss them so much that there is a great big hole in the pit of my stomach that nothing can fill. I literally feel my heart hurt, and there's nothing I can do. Because of that, I wanted to come to share with you a little bit about the world your loved ones are living in right now so I can help narrow the distance between Peoria, Illinois, and Vietnam for you.

"First, let's talk about what there is in Vietnam that you don't have: the rainy season. Vietnam has two seasons: the sunny season and the rainy season. In the rainy season it may not rain constantly, but it rains every day. Humidity at times can be so stifling that you can't breathe. Though with the rain comes a cleansing of the earth and the air. The sunny season is miserably hot and there's no relief with rain. At times there is no breeze. So that's a contrast that your family member is experiencing. No white Christmas, and no snow. Everything is brown and green all year-long, depending on the season: green from the leaves and grasses in the forest, and brown from the dirt and rocks.

"The food they eat is also very different than what you are used to here. Vietnam doesn't have a lot of grazing grounds, so little meat is available. Beef is imported from Australia, though it's rare. The local people mostly eat chicken and pork as they can raise them locally. Chickens walk all around, and even through the houses. Fruits are plentiful and part of the common diet.

"One thing that children don't see much of is hair, like hair on arms. Most people in

Vietnam have little hair, so the children find it funny to see and will actually pull on arm hair of visitors! It makes the children laugh and the visitors as well.

"Something that gave me a lot of comfort when I came to the United States was when people looked at me and smiled. Simple as it is, it made my world better and meant so much to me. Please know this: the Vietnamese people love Americans. So when your family members who are there meet the locals, they will get big welcoming smiles and know that they are appreciated."

I wasn't conscious of it at the time, but I was already called to bridge the gap of communication between cultures. It wasn't me who the women were angry at, but the situation that had ensnared their loved ones. They didn't know the country where they were and were unable to visualize them. Through my descriptions, I was able to provide them with that peace.

Years later, while working in corporate America for a Fortune 100 company, I had a business trip to India. My boss was supposed to go because we were dealing with some resistance in the diversity team toward taking the diversity strategy, including education, to India. This resistance was lost in translation, and the headquarters for my company took it as a personality clash. In fact, it was actually cultural resistance to the changes and the methods of deployment.

As a business, sometimes we forget that every location has its own culture and operates accordingly. When strategies are created in headquarters, we share information with our global locations and expect them to deploy the same way across the enterprise. This could create a resistance because we don't want to be told what do to.

My boss couldn't go to this meeting in India, so I went in his place. The group that I met was rather cold. Twenty-six people in the senior leadership team, from the plant manager to the department heads, joined me in the room. Tension and distrust were clearly felt.

In India, the rule of hospitality is that as guests, people would have been all over us trying to make us comfortable and to feel welcomed. However, we were not. The hospitality was not visible at all and the environment was starkly cold. People looked straight at me with no expression.

I glanced around the room and decided to begin the meeting. "Good morning," I said. No one moved. No one reacted or responded. I looked around and then put my hands together and lightly bowed, saying, "Namaste," and repeating it to every side of the room. By the time I finished, the feeling in the room had completely changed. People nodded in welcome, and the look that they gave me was no longer one of hostility, but of welcome. My vision was greeted by smiles. *Namaste* is a traditional greeting in India and Nepal, representing the respect and humility of the greeter with the meaning: "the god in me greets the god in you."

I said, "I apologize on behalf of my boss and of the CEO of our company, who wanted to come but could not, and sent me in his stead. On behalf of my boss and on behalf of the CEO, I greet each one of you in their name and thank you for being here." Americans don't usually think much about business protocol when we do business with other countries, especially if the people we are interacting with speak English as well.

Every country has a certain protocol. When we don't know the protocol, at best, we may be ignored. At worst, people may take offense to what we do or don't do. Understanding protocol and culture makes great strides toward helping us achieve our business goals successfully.

A little humility goes a long way. My colleagues in India accepted me because I spoke on behalf of the people of authority. I humbled myself with the apology and it was accepted generously, neutralizing the resistance and resolving the conflict.

This can be a challenge as in America as the cultural norm is not to apologize unless a person does something wrong. However, in other cultures, an apology is not admitting fault but a show of humility. Coming from a colonized country as Vietnam was and India was, I understood that people from headquarters should not go to India and tell the people there what to do. I sensed humility was what was needed and provided it. I realized how critically important it was to secure buy-in from the local branch in the new direction.

Positioning is so important in cross-cultural discussions. The people in India had the autonomy to manage their people at their location, so I was there to serve them and not to tell them what to do. The culture in India is hierarchical, and the people in power locally earned their place and the right of authority there. So it was important for me to recognize their power. By bringing the apology from my boss, I did that. I validated them to show the appropriate respect, and because of that I was able to get their buy-in on the strategy and then inspire them to take the action that they needed to take.

In my work, it doesn't matter where I go. My mission follows me in support of any plan or business strategy. My personal mission, what I believe in so strongly, always goes with me. I practice it everywhere and it serves me well. Through recognition, validation, education and communication, this process helps me to achieve my business goals and allows me to define success in my life.

Chapter 6

Knowledge and Respect

Sometimes the best way to recognize similarities in people is to acknowledge the differences. Communication is critical when establishing new relationships, and it's so important to not make assumptions about people based on cultural norms or expectations.

I went to Mexico City to facilitate a workshop. Class was scheduled from 9 a.m. to 5 p.m. As a facilitator, I arrived early to set up and to make sure that I was prepared. As an American, arriving early demonstrated the importance of this workshop to me.

The scheduled start time of the class came and went, and no one arrived. Ten o'clock came and went, and no one arrived. Eleven o'clock came and went, and no one arrived.

As a diversity leader, I had facilitated many workshops on cultural differences, so I was prepared. I brought work to do and books to read. Even so, after a couple of hours, my mind started racing with anxious thoughts: Did I come on the wrong date? Why was no one arriving? Did they not want to attend the class?

People started to arrive at 11:45. When they came in, I thought, "How will I get all of the material done in five hours?" I greeted the attendees, and they started to talk. No one seemed eager to start class! They asked me how my trip was, where I was coming from, and how the weather was there. Since they asked me questions, I had to ask them similar questions to show they were important to me.

After the questions, I thanked them for their hospitality and said that it was wonderful. However, I stated I had a challenge that required their help. All eyes in the room faced me, eagerly waiting to know how they could be of assistance to me. "We have an eight-hour workshop, and I don't know how to get it all done in this short time," I said. They all wanted to help, and declared that I should not worry and that we would be able to do it.

I had the best workshop of my career that day. We left at 9:45 p.m. I received the most memorable and meaningful compliment that I had ever received after class when they took me to dinner.

One of the attendees said, "Christine, you may not know this, but we were watching you."

"You were? When?" I said.

We were watching you to see whether or not you were upset because we were not here at 9:00 as it says on the schedule."

"No, I wasn't upset," I said.

"We know! We saw you and saw that you weren't upset. It was as if you knew we would come when we were ready."

I told them, "I came here to serve you. So whenever you are ready, I will do so."

They questioned me, "Just like that?" I didn't have any choice, certainly, and they knew what they were doing.

"So how did I do?" I asked. I was told that day that I was their hero. No presenter had ever done that—just sat patiently and waited for them to arrive. They told me they had watched leaders who got upset, who raged, and who left. However, I didn't. They said they had watched me and knew that I knew what I was doing. The workshop was about diversity, and I showed that I knew what I was doing by showing them respect. I demonstrated it, and through that earned their respect and gained credibility.

"Thank you for honoring me with your presence and active participation, allowing me to learn with you," I said, and meant it.

As an American, showing up that late shows a marked disrespect. Respect means the same thing worldwide; however, it is expressed very differently. Understanding this, I was quite frustrated by their lateness but knew what was happening and was prepared for it. Culture is an amazing thing, and when you know about it and understand, it can turn out beautifully.

It is important to understand that we are all different. Even if we look alike, sound alike, and define ourselves in similar ways, we are all very different individuals. Dialogue is important to understand each other, and to show an appreciation and proper respect for who we are. People are unique individuals, so we cannot make assumptions. Stereotype and bias are what comes naturally to us as we try to define or categorize the world around us. We don't think about it, but it's how we are taught.

Chapter 7

Corporate and Beyond

Diversity work often comes with the challenge of helping people to understand what it really is. Beyond just the definition of diversity, working in this field also requires the ability to probe to reach the underlying issues, a high level of sensitivity and respect, and the patience to be able to work with people over the long term.

People often can clearly articulate their challenges; however, they don't always see that their issue may be part of a larger opportunity to integrate diversity and inclusion into the workplace. For example, at one company, women were unable to apply for certain jobs because the position required the person work late into the night and leadership did not want to put a woman in that position. Other companies will not consider a woman for a position with significant travel due to a belief that it's not right for them. This could be viewed as taking care of the people working at the company, but on the other hand, it's making an assumption as to a woman's ability to perform a specific job.

In Korea, a woman must stop working when she gets pregnant, regardless of the position she works in. In Mexico, men are often seen in leadership roles as team leaders and department heads, as that is the cultural norm. This is part of the country culture, however, it could be challenging with hiring and retention.

Diversity has its place in a corporate environment, providing that we stay focused on respect for the individual and what he or she wants and needs to get the job done. When does something become a diversity issue? When the individual cannot make a decision for themselves about their ability and capability to perform a task or job.

When there is corporate buy-in for diversity initiatives, it is often met with success. One company that I worked for decided to drive a diversity initiative, and they showed the importance of the initiative by tying 25 percent of the employee bonus to it. Diversity was then considered part of the business operation and was taken much more seriously. It enabled me to incorporate the strategy tied to those diversity initiatives, and people were interested in knowing what they could do to achieve their full bonus payout.

Companies can leverage significant opportunities by recognizing diversity. At one large company I worked for, a Hispanic employee network was created and was leveraged to help the company translate employment applications into Spanish to load on the corporate website for Latin American countries. This group also assisted with recommendations regarding local customs: what to say, what not to say, and who was required to get things done.

The same company had some issues in France due to a misunderstanding of cultural differences with the offices in the United States. The French office thought the Americans were being arrogant; however, the issue was more a lack of understanding and different communication styles.

I worked through issues similar to the ones I mentioned about India earlier—where the office in India had concerns about people from the corporate headquarters dictating business decisions when they generally had a significant level of autonomy—in other countries like Hong Kong, Singapore, and Australia. In order to demonstrate respect and the importance of bridging the challenges, I established conference calls done at a time convenient to those I was working with in other countries. This simple act of respect was recognized and appreciated.

As a "cultural interpreter," an endearing title given me by my global colleagues, I established structure to enable recognition of diversity initiatives. I was brought in as a consultant to mediate and provided training and education. As part of the role, I often helped with the roll-out of global strategy to offices and helped them translate that strategy to their particular business and function.

On September 11, 2001, the terrorist attack on the United States impacted everyone in the country, whether directly or indirectly. After the dust settled, everyone struggled to make sense of the event, and businesses struggled as well with how to reinvigorate the economy.

It was around the same time that I read a horrible story about a child in England who was bludgeoned to death by a six-year-old and his friend for no reason other than he had a disability. It hit me hard as three of my four grandsons lived with autism. I became fearful of the world they would grow up in and wanted to do something to make a difference in their lives and the lives around me. I wanted to channel my fear into something positive and productive.

This prompted action, and I organized a round table meeting for the business, education, and government communities to join together to discuss their struggles and successful best practices, and to share available resources to make a difference. There was a cross-section of people in leadership roles, including ninety-seven people representing twenty-nine companies. The first meeting was in early 2002 at the Phoenix Botanical Garden. The agenda included topics like:

- What are your struggles in terms of diversity?
- What are your resources?

- What are you/is your company good at in your diversity practice?
- What challenges do you see, and how can we work together to achieve success?
- Sharing of best practices

People were inspired and motivated, and the call to action was heard. From that day forward, we began a strong partnership amongst the community that is being celebrated regularly. The second annual meeting included three hundred people representing close to seventy companies. The Diversity Leadership Alliance (DLA) was born.

The DLA's mission is to guide leaders in the transformation of a culture to build an inclusive community. We focus on providing education so people can learn to accept all people. It ties closely to what I want for my grandchildren: to offer everyone the same rights to thrive, even if they are not perfect. To this end, a focus on youth was added in 2004 to reach the next generation. A youth strategy was developed to work with school districts to reach high school students, helping them transition from school to higher education and adulthood. Monthly student workshops are offered to provide education and practical tools, and these are attended by more than one hundred people each month.

The Diversity Leadership Alliance (DLA) also offers consultation services, benchmarking, and an ability to network at regularly-scheduled events. The power of DLA is in the understanding the membership has that people and companies are not successful alone. All members contribute to the success of the group through the sharing of knowledge, resources, and experience.

Now approaching its tenth annual conference, the same companies that were in the original group are represented, joined by many others. At more than 2,000 participants strong, the DLA offers monthly workshops at no cost to educate people on diversity issues to help them live in a more inclusive environment and to help them promote and manage the understanding of diversity in their surroundings. Members take ownership in creating this positive environment. Monthly workshops are attended by more than 150 people and include topics like:

- Micro-inequities: subtle ways we show value and respect, and the meaning behind our actions that we may or may not recognize
- Working with multi-generations
- Working with disability
- Employee engagement
- Personal leadership
- Working effectively across cultures

As the founder and president of the organization, I am very direct about my vision for the future. The Diversity Leadership Alliance's (DLA) vision is "to be an inclusive community where each individual is equally respected and empowered." My hope is essentially that there is no longer a need for DLA in the future. There's such strong support from every level in the community to drive the vision so that everyone will be equally respected and empowered. When that is realized, there will no longer be a need for the Diversity Leadership Alliance (DLA).

The success of the DLA would not happen without the dedication and commitment of my colleague and co-chair, Marion Kelly from Mayo Clinic. Marion was one of the first colleagues who responded to the call for the Diversity Leadership round table in 2002. Marion and I have been co-chairing the DLA since then.

I am grateful to be gifted with a good friend, loyal supporter, and brilliant partner in the building of an inclusive community.

As we celebrate the tenth anniversary of the formation of the DLA this year, the organization looks to draw more youths and people working with youths to drive the vision into the future. Providing young people with a firm foundation on which to stand and drive change in terms of inclusion and equality are critical to the mission of the organization. This work gives me the hope that my grandsons will live in a society where they don't have to worry about being beaten for not being perfect. And everyone's children in the future will be able to live in a safe, supportive, and nurturing community.

I'm now working to form a new nonprofit to provide music education and instruction to children living with autism. Having seen how my grandsons really connect with music, I'm passionate about this project. It gives them something positive to enjoy, to be good at, and to focus on. They are transformed when performing, and I want to spread that joy that I see on their faces to others who can benefit from it. I'm working to recruit music teachers who will donate their time to working with children living with autism to help them achieve the same joy that I see in my own grandsons.

Chapter 8

Awards and
Acknowledgments

Throughout the years, I've received recognition for my diversity work, which I humbly accept in honor of my Father, the one who gave me everything I need and taught me everything I know. The recognition is really for all of my diversity colleagues and countless people who work tirelessly to ensure everyone is equally respected and empowered. It validates the importance of the work that we do in diversity and inclusion. Acknowledgment of the importance and the power of diversity and inclusion cultivates an environment where innovative ideas are ignited, resulting in new products and services.

No one is successful alone, and I so greatly appreciate the dedication of the many incredible people devoted to the cause of spreading an understanding of the power of diversity and inclusion. At the end of the day, through this recognition, this humble woman felt so tall and so big because she had the privilege of standing on the shoulders of the many giants who have walked before her and beside her! Following are a few of the awards I've accepted on behalf of the work that I was called to do.

I was recognized by the Arizona Society of Human Resource Management (SHRM) and awarded the Workforce Diversity Champion in 2004, both for my work done in Arizona with the Diversity Leadership Alliance as well as my work in corporate positions.

In 2006, I received the YWCA Tribute to Women award in the Racial Justice category, recognizing my work in field of diversity. This annual award is given to ten recipients who are recognized for their work and devotion to a special cause.

Additionally, in 2006 the *Arizona Business Journal* wrote a series on influential women in business, and I received a Women in Business Award.

In 2010, I was nominated for the Athena Award. This international honor recognizes exemplary achievements and seeks to inspire others to achieve excellence in their professional and personal lives. More than five thousand awards have been presented since the program's inception in 1982. The winners are women who:

- Assist or mentor women to reach their full leadership potential
- Demonstrate excellence, creativity, and initiative in their profession
- Provide valuable service by devoting consistent and continuous time and energy to improve the lives of others

It is an honor and a privilege to receive these acknowledgments; however, it's not really about me. It is about the recognition of the work that I have the privilege of being a part of and the importance of recognizing the value of diversity and inclusion in work and in life. It is also an affirmation that ALL of us have a need to be equally respected and empowered.

Chapter 9

Learning from Mistakes

Making mistakes is a natural path of life. It's one of the steps we make toward the achievement of our goals, and while many of us wish we would not make any mistakes, it really is a necessary step. As much as we dislike it, try to avoid it, and deny it, our mistakes guide us toward learning and growing. When we are fully aware that much of our success depends on how well we learn from our mistakes, then we can be more open to look at the mistakes, examine them, learn from them, and explore the variety of ways we could do things differently to achieve our goals.

I have made my share of mistakes in both my personal and professional life. Following is a sample of the mistakes I've made, and most importantly, the lessons they taught me.

Fear Takes the Reins

All of my corporate jobs have been extended to me without my actively pursuing them. Somehow each time, people have heard of me, invited me in for interviews, and extended me the job. Several years ago, I was offered a diversity manager position with a Fortune 100 company, working with a team of eight people from various cultural backgrounds. Our team members were sprinkled around the United States and included African-Americans, Latinas, Asians, gays and lesbians, people with disabilities, and Caucasians—all between the ages of twenty-nine and sixty-five. We worked well together, and we each sat in a different region of the country. The team spoke every week on a conference call, and met face-to-face at headquarters every other month. Our weekly conference calls were lively with the sharing of activities we all did in our respective areas. Most people excitedly talked about their accomplishments, asking each other about their projects to learn from their successes and failures.

Being new to the team, my primary task was to build relationships with my business leaders and strategic partners throughout the organization, and my time was mostly spent in meetings getting to know my client groups in order to better serve them. Certainly, I could have used a lot of help from my teammates and would have greatly benefitted from their introduction to these leaders. I might have more quickly learned about their businesses to position my team as a strategic partner, which would have cemented the relationships within my team and with my team and other parts of the organization. However, I didn't ask for help and was cautious not to ask too many questions and not to volunteer too many ideas and opinions. When my colleagues asked if there was anything they could do for me, I was always politely said, "Thank you for offering, but I am doing fine. As a matter of fact, everything is going very well."

I was guided by my Asian culture not to ask questions. I learned as a child that it was not good to reveal your weaknesses to others. I was taught to accept my responsibilities fully: I needed to learn them, own them, and not depend on others for help. Being the newest member of the team, I wanted to make sure that my leader did not think they chose the wrong person, so I said very little about anything. In the team meetings, I was careful not to offer my ideas and opinions just in case I might be wrong or, worse yet, because they might not like what I had to say and would reject me.

I thought I did a good job keeping my insecurities under wraps. In actuality, all I really accomplished was creating confusion and distrust within my team, especially with my African-American colleague. I didn't know at the time, but in the African-American culture, silence, or lack of response, is seen as a sign of disrespect. My team thought I was stuck-up and disrespectful because I did not accept their offer to help and did not share my opinions when they asked. You might think that because we were members of a diversity team, we would have known all there was to know about how to work effectively with people who were different than us. I sure had a lot to learn then.

Eventually, I did open up to my colleagues and asked for help. By then, so much time had been wasted, so much trust had been squandered, and so many opportunities had been missed. It took so much longer for me to build the trust with my colleagues because of how I approached them and because I didn't understand the impact of both what I said and did as well as what I did not say and do. Needless to say, my team did not reach the level of productivity that a high-performing team would have.

At my six-month performance review, I received a so-so assessment from my team leader, who cited my lack of teamwork and engagement with the group. I was devastated and realized that I needed help. I reached out to a friend and mentor who coached me on effective communication and personal leadership.

Reaching out to ask for help and being open to making changes based on the recommendations I received set me on the right path toward making amends with my team. I learned to take risks, ask questions when I needed clarifications, and manage my fear rather than let it manage me. I was often amazed by how accepting people were when I asked questions; no one ever got mad at me for asking them and no one ever told me I was stupid when I admitted I did not know how to do certain things. Slowly, as I learned to trust my colleagues, they reciprocated by offering their trust as well. Eventually, we did become one of the high-performing teams, breaking many of the records in the company.

Our culture is a precious thing. However, a lack of understanding about how our cultural tendencies are perceived by others can keep us from learning, growing, and achieving our goals. Awareness of our cultural tendencies and the implication of them, as well as those of others, helps us to be more effective in situations where we interact with people from different backgrounds. When we dialogue with people from different cultural backgrounds, we learn about each others' culture, ways of thinking, and wants and needs, and we expand our perspective and enrich our thought process.

Once the communication began steadily flowing, our team made a commitment to each other to listen without judgment. We also learned to seek each other's ideas and perspective to better serve our client groups. It was amazing to find out that as we trusted each other more, we enjoyed our work so much more, and we celebrated each other's success as if it was our own.

Trust Goes Awry

Most of us have had challenges with a manager at one time or another. Sometimes we know right away whether our manager is effective, and other times it takes some time to learn just how ineffective—or even hurtful—that person can be.

After an organization that I worked for was restructured, I reported to a new manager who came from another company. The first three months were like a courting period of sorts. Everyone was pleasant to each other, trying to find out about each other and to determine how best to work effectively together. We had off-site strategy meetings with playtime built in as we were building a new team.

My new boss called me to her office one day, telling me how impressed she was with my performance and maturity, and how much she enjoyed seeing the positive results of my leadership. This made me feel good. I believed I could trust her and thought we would have a successful career together. What I didn't know at the time was that she had had the same conversation with the rest of the team as well. It was the start of what was to come.

In our one-on-one weekly meetings thereafter, everything would go well and our discussions were all very positive. Then one time as the meeting was ending, she said, "May I ask you something personal?"

"Of course," I said, because I trusted her then.

"How well do you work with Mindy?" she asked.

I replied that we worked together very well, and asked why she wanted to know.

She hesitated and then said, "Well, I think Mindy is jealous of you, because she tried to discredit you for your work on the project. Please don't say anything just in case I misread her."

Normally, I would call Mindy to ask what that was all about, but because my boss, whom I trusted, asked me not to say anything, I didn't. Then I noticed that Mindy was kind of cold toward me. She hardly said anything to me at meetings and avoided my eye contact. Her behavior made me think my boss was right about Mindy, so I kept my distance from her as well.

Slowly but surely, a sense of coldness and distrust brewed among the team members. We said less and less to each other and in time communicated only with the boss. This went on for around six months until one day, when our boss was on vacation, we had to deliver on a project and needed information from everyone on the team. We scheduled a conference call to pull the information together for this project. At first everyone cautiously talked about the project and then one person spoke up. "What's going on? We haven't talked with each other in months. Whatever's going on, we can handle it as a team…"

That's all it took, and just as if someone poked a pin into a water balloon, everyone in the room got wet. Team members started to challenge each other about what the boss had said to each of us. In an instant, we all realized what had happened, and right then and there our team came back together with the commitment to each other's success, working together again. Our team once again became a high-performing team.

This experience taught me to listen more carefully and to start asking questions when things I hear from a third person don't seem to line up with what I know of that person. A good friend shared this very helpful and insightful acronym with me that we need to THINK before we speak.

THINK is an acronym for:

T: is it true?

H: is it helpful?

I: is it important?

N: is it necessary?

K: is it kind?

When we talk with each other, it is easy and tempting to say something negative about someone we don't particularly like. So when I take the time to THINK, it is that much easier to take the high road and to not give in to the temptation of offering my opinion without considering the consequence or value of doing so.

The Downside of Pride

Though pride can be a feeling of self-respect and personal worth, its misperception can bring about animosity among team members, causing issues with the productivity of any business unit. I hope the sharing of my mistakes will lead you to take a proactive role in preventing them.

When I was offered the job as the new global marketing manager for a Fortune 100 company, I was so happy and grateful to have the opportunity to work with team members in Asia, Europe, North America, and Latin America. As a child, I had always dreamed of being an ambassador to clarify communications with people from other nations and to spread understanding and goodwill from my home country. In this role, I was able to take communications from Chicago, the company headquarters, to various countries in these regions to clarify and bridge the cultural understanding among various business units as we worked toward the company's goals. I was so excited about all that I could do in this role and proud that it was offered to me.

I was in my element: I loved the work and thoroughly enjoyed the people as I worked tirelessly to ensure the global team's success. Our global team members appreciated being briefed on what was going on at headquarters, and I was able to explain the nuances of the language and cultural differences. Each member was able to identify and take ownership of the portion of the goal they were responsible for. The work and productivity of our division went through the roof, as members of our global team felt valued and appreciated when they saw that headquarters cared enough to send a representative to personally share the information and business strategies to several layers of the organization rather than just the department heads. Leadership effectiveness, employee engagement, and cross-team training were at an all-time high.

The positive response from the global team members energized me and inspired me to want to serve them more. Besides, I was in my element. I got to be the division's ambassador, and I loved to see our team be so successful. My Asian heritage helped me connect with the Asian team members easily, and the European team accepted me quickly when they discovered that I could speak French. Our division enjoyed the highest productivity and profit in the sector, and everyone was proud to be part of this success.

I was shocked to learn that not everyone was happy. A couple of the division's general managers' direct reports were very angry and demanded that I be removed from the global team. After all, no one gave me permission to hold meetings with various levels in the organization, especially with these folks' peers in Asia, Europe, and Latin America. They felt I had stepped into their territories without permission, making them look bad. In reality, the global team thought that since their general manager sent me, they were free to ask for my support, and they appreciated the opportunity to meet in person rather than via teleconference.

Our general manager caved under constant pressure from his direct reports even though he was the one sending me to support the global team. He asked me to not attend the next quarterly global team meeting, giving his direct reports a chance to cool down a bit. The plan backfired big-time. When the team gathered in France for the quarterly meeting, global team members were looking for me. When our general manager said he asked me not to attend, several of them got upset. They told him about all the things I had done, saying that I was the person responsible for the division's success and that they were disappointed he did not value me as he should.

Back in Phoenix, I received a phone call from my general manager asking me to join them in France the next day. It was a little uncomfortable for me to be warmly welcomed by the global team members while I knew there were people who did not want me there. After the global meeting, I tried to set up meetings with the folks who had issues with me to talk things out, but there was no interest on their part. They felt I had gone out of my way to make them look bad. Their perception was that I was showing off my cultural background and language ability to the global team, that I had brainwashed everybody, and that the division's success was due to their leadership and not anything to do with my contribution.

The pride I have for myself and my respect for the global team would not allow me to change the level of support I provided to them. However, the constant criticism sapped my energy and took much of my pleasure out of the job. When a job offer presented itself a couple of months later, I took it just to be out of this negative environment.

I made several mistakes in this situation. With the experience and maturity that I have today, I certainly would have done things differently. I have always felt I made a mistake leaving the job I truly loved just to be out of the negative environment. I should have stayed with the job and not allowed a couple of people to sap my energy and ruin the pleasure I got from what I was doing. By leaving, I gave up the opportunity to work with wonderful people who appreciated me and with whom I enjoyed working. I also gave up my power to the people who did not care about me instead of keeping that power to serve my friends and colleagues. I should not have walked away when these people were not interested in meeting with me. Today I would have engaged a mediator to resolve this conflict to break the cycle of retaliation, as I did not have any ill will toward them.

Another mistake I made was at the beginning of the assignment. Upon receiving the order from the general manager to support the global team, I should have requested meetings with each of his direct supports to build relationships, providing opportunities for me to get to know them and for them to get to know me so they wouldn't feel as if I was invading their territory. Today I would have taken the opportunity to do some team building with them in order to cultivate an inclusive culture and trust among the general manager's direct reports.

I missed the boat several times when I did not humble myself and invite them to the meetings with the global team. I was too busy enjoying my new and exciting job that I missed opportunities to draw these folks in so they would take ownership of the work instead of feeling I was competing with them. Through this situation, I learned a lesson in order to achieve business success: we need to build partnership with everyone and engage others in all activities to share the responsibilities and results alike. This way, we will get the buy-in from all the players and will not have to face the wrath of some competitive souls in the organization.

Going With Your Gut

Shortly after the start-up of our consulting business, I was working hard to develop the business by meeting with potential clients and assessing their business state to recommend an improvement plan. Quite often, we would get a call from an organization wanting us to provide some training. Our typical response would be to request a meeting with these folks to determine the reason for their training need, assess the organization's level of readiness, and then develop a customized training plan for them.

A few years back, we received an RFP from a midsized organization with a request for a complex training plan. We were really excited to have the opportunity to create a whole system of learning for this organization. We submitted the RFP and were awarded the contract shortly thereafter.

We did the usual: we met with members of the organization's leadership team as well as with the training team to learn about their culture, their processes, their challenges, and their needs. Our team members and I were totally committed to making this the best experience for everyone, both our organization and the client's organization. We were eating, sleeping, and breathing the project.

A couple of months later, our training program was ready and we were very excited to deliver the first training in a series of ten sessions. This was a mandatory training session for all of our client's staff; senior leaders, team members, front line workers, and everyone else attended the session together. While attendees from the lower levels of the organization really appreciated and enjoyed the workshop, it was clear the organization's leadership did not. As part of workshop interaction, we facilitated many activities requiring participants to change seats so people would have the opportunity to interface with many people they might not have had a chance to meet or did not work with regularly. Some of the members of the leadership team started to talk, telling jokes during the workshop and disrupting others.

Evaluations from workshop participants were high across the board, yet the "organizing team" wanted to meet to give us their own feedback separately. Since customer satisfaction is one of our consulting company's main priorities, we eagerly looked for their feedback to ensure we met their expectations and to practice our continuous improvement plan.

Taking the customer's feedback from all levels of the organization, our team eagerly revised the training modules, and again, we were excited to have a product we were so proud of. To our dismay, the feedback from the leadership team was largely negative, with comments like: "too much information," "we heard of that before," and "we are not learning anything new." A lot of time and conversation went on between the client and our team, and in the end, we decided to withdraw the contract, feeling that continuing would be like "beating a dead horse."

All of the effort, time, resources, and goodwill on the part of our consulting firm seemed to go unappreciated, and it was clear we would not meet with this client's leadership team's approval. This was probably one of the hardest and most painful lessons my team and I learned.

Some of what we learned from this experience includes:

1. Leadership buy-in is essential to the success of any program. In this case, we were told the leadership supported the training plan. Our understanding was that

we needed to meet with as many leaders as possible to gauge their understanding and buy-in prior to the work.

2. As consultants, we have a tendency to want to please the client. However, sometimes it is necessary for us to stand firm in our conviction. When this client told us they wanted to have everyone attend the workshop series, including senior leaders, department heads, team leaders, staff, and team members to ensure everyone heard the same thing, we should have insisted on having a separate session with the leaders and department heads. We knew that even if everyone needed to hear the same message, different levels of the organization needed to learn different things. Leaders needed to learn about the plan, the processes, and the pay-off to manage the team's performance while the staff and team members needed to learn the tools, acquire the skills to execute the plan, and work the processes to achieve

the pay-off. Instead of insisting that the most effective means of learning for each of the groups would be to train them separately, we gave in to their insistence on keeping everyone together, to the detriment of the learning process.

3. As consultants working outside of our client's organization, we needed to remember the reason we got the job: clients engaged us because of our expertise, knowledge, skills, and credibility. We needed to listen to what clients wanted, to explore the challenges they faced, and to assess their needs and readiness prior to preparing a proposal for the improvement plan. Quite often clients will tell us what they want, assessing their own needs without letting us do the assessment for their readiness, as in this case.

Our learning is nowhere finished for this BIG lesson. As we strive for continuous improvement, we will continue to find nuggets of wisdom in similar situations to help us better serve our clients in the future.

Understanding Politics

One of the things I learned early in life is: it's ALL about relationships. Whether we work in a small organization or a large one, non-profit or corporate, as a volunteer or a business owner, we cannot be successful without building good relationships with those around us. This is particularly the case with our internal customers. This sounds simple enough, but real-life situations are anything but simple. Following is a sample of my mistakes on this topic.

Early in my career, I was a technical trainer for a large manufacturing company. I had great relationships with my peers, other trainers, and especially the workers whom I was responsible for training. These relationships made my job fun and fulfilling as I enjoyed making a difference in my world of work.

Basking in the warm friendship of the line workers, I did notice the team leaders would not talk with me. Because I assumed they didn't like me, I stopped going to them with information, news, and changes impacting them and instead communicated directly with the line workers. The team leaders obviously did not appreciate this, and I noticed things started to go wrong for me.

I missed an important meeting with the head of manufacturing because somehow the invitation did not get to me until the day after the meeting. I was scheduled to teach a class for the first shift and the second shift of the same day, and an hour before this class ended I was told I needed to teach the third-shift class, making for a twenty-four-hour day. Incidents like this continued happening, and in my ignorance of the corporate silent rules, I thought it was a coincidence. My attitude was that if people needed training on a new process, I needed to deliver. Besides, I would do anything for my line workers because I believed they were the most important people in the business. Without their work, the company would not have had products to sell, and without good products, the business would not be successful.

A few weeks later, there was an opening for the training head. Of course all of my line workers encouraged me to apply because they all knew I was qualified for it. So I did, and I did not even get an interview for the job! They hired someone from outside who did not know anything about our line of work, and I had to report to him.

This news served as a wake-up call for me, and my friends from the line confirmed I would not get anywhere in that environment. My friends further educated me on the "business protocol"—that no one bypassed the team leaders and survived professionally. Wow! What a painful lesson that was! I learned then, and continue to learn even today, that regardless of a person's position or profession, we need to build relationships with EVERYONE in the business. Of course we don't have to like everybody; we just need to know who they are, learn to work with them, and support them to the best of our abilities if we want to be successful. You never know who is truly important or powerful.

Since then, I made a point of creating a process map for each job or assignment I have with all the people I need to connect with to get the job done. I believe relationship building is one of the most important aspects to achieving our goals, both personally and professionally.

Summary

My diversity work is not about changing the world but getting people to think about their own actions and the consequences. I encourage people to ask questions: Why are we doing this? What is the benefit? Is it necessary and important? Does it make sense? And of course, is it kind? Thinking before we act and before we speak could make a huge difference in our environment, making our world a lot more pleasant, enjoyable, and healthy.

Disagreement can make a person feel invalidated, like they've been judged, and ego can get in the way of bringing forward some wonderful new ideas. So it's important to me to remain open to listening and to learning.

My in-laws accepted me for who I was and loved me for it. Their love and generosity really made a difference in my life and is one of the many lessons I have learned and will cherish always. When my daughter was born, my husband's boss' wife, Mary Lee, helped me tremendously by visiting with food, doing laundry, and helping me clean. She took my daughter and me for drives so we were not stuck in the apartment all day. Why? She did it because it was kind and because she wanted to. I learned and trusted that she was helping me out of the goodness of her heart, as she truly had no reason to otherwise.

Diversity was not discussed when I was younger, but I learned at a very young age how powerful it can be. Where people ordinarily may have questioned my motives, they often trusted that I was truly passionate about my work and wanted to help. I have made mistakes along the way, which is good. My goal is not to never make mistakes but to always learn from them.

As an adult, my childhood shaped me in many ways. I learned from the experience on my first day of school that I would be much more successful when I followed the following rules: know yourself, know the people around you, know your business, and know your environment. Regardless of our feelings, it's critical to really understand what's going on around us so we can respond properly rather than just react. My mother taught me when I was young that you can say anything to anybody, but the difference is in knowing when and how to do so.

Last November I ran a workshop at an educational institution. The dean behaved in a patronizing manner toward me as I didn't have a Ph.D. and the credentials that he expected I would have. I didn't look like I belonged and didn't appear to fit in the environment, so I was not readily accepted. I see this often, as it's expected that people doing the work I've done will be in a higher position than me. They don't often expect a small woman to come walking in the room and share the experiences I have had!

Following my presentation, the dean reached out to me. He mentioned he was in the Vietnam War and later shared pictures with me of his time in the military. Once he met me and heard what I had to say, I became a person. It's so important to me to provide that validation to others and to accept them, understanding how it feels on the receiving end. It's important to maintain our own identity; however, we must also recognize and respect the differences of others.

Diversity is the expression of life, and this is the life I have been given.

I have my whole life to prove that the power of love and respect will win over the powers of hate and prejudice. The world becomes a better place when we all start to look at things differently. Through our own personal definition of diversity, we can drive our own success and the success of those around us. My life can be proof of the success that we can weave, personally and professionally, when we are open to it. It's not about us not making mistakes, but in learning from them in order to continue our process of development and growth. It benefits us, it benefits the people and organizations around us, and it benefits the world.

Abe Lincoln once said, "I don't like that man. I must get to know him better." Who would have thought that Abraham Lincoln would be such a wise practitioner of diversity?